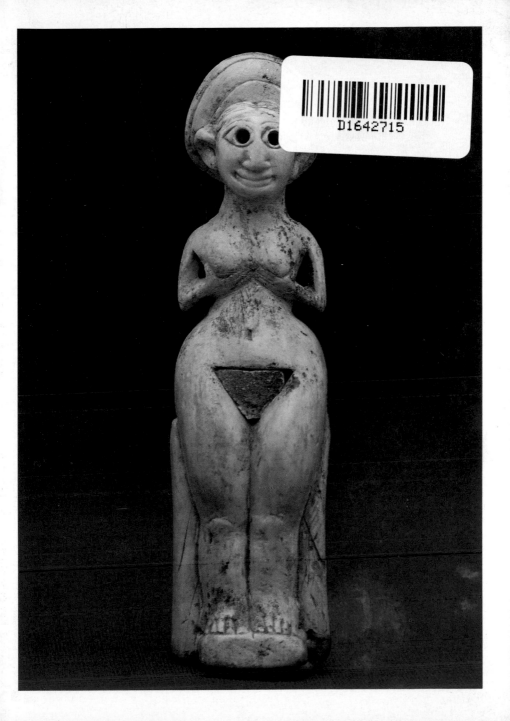

THE HITTITES

TAHSİN ÖZGÜÇ

THE HITTITES

By the second half of the third millennium BC, a highly developed civilisation was already in existence in Anatolia. City principalities had been established and the country was governed according to a feudal system. Anatolian civilisation at that time was characterised by a high level of craftsmanship in metals of all kinds. In recognition of this fact, the Assyrians, who had been settled in northern Mesopotamia since around the year 2000 BC, established large trading colonies, especially in the area between Malatya and Konya. Assyrian merchants brought tin and textiles and ready-made materials such as clothes from Assyria by donkey caravans of 200 - 250 donkeys, and sold them to the local inhabitants at high prices, in exchange for gold and silver. The Assyrians had to pay taxes imposed by the local princes, who in return ensured the security necessary for trade to be conducted. Apart from their trade relations, the Assyrians had no political or administrative influence over the hereditary princes or the indigenous people. Most of the population were made up of the autochthonous inhabitants of the land of Hatti, whose language belonged neither to the Indo - European nor the Semitic family of languages. The most important development of the era of the Assyrian trading colonies was the fact that the Assyrian merchants introduced them for the first time to the cuneiform script

and to the Assyrian language. In this way, the prehistoric period in Anatolia came to an end, the land entered into the light of history, and Anatolia opened its doors to the most highly civilised parts of the ancient world and established links with them. The kingdom of Kanish was the first state to feature in the history of relations between Mesopotamia and Anatolia. The two major regions of the ancient civilised world came into close contact in this area.

At that time, the inhabitants of Anatolia not only learned how to write and to operate an extensively organised system of trade and public administration, but also increased the level of their own art and culture through contact with the highly developed art of the old, civilised world. During this period, the Hittites, who spoke an Indo-European language, began to migrate to Anatolia, at first slowly and in groups, and later on with increasing power, capturing one important city after another. In this way, they began to exert their dominance over the real owners of the country, the Hatti. When the Hittites first came to Anatolia, they had nothing in the way of progressive civilisation with which to influence the indigenous inhabitants, apart from their language. However, the Hittites managed to adapt to the indigenous culture and make it their own. Strictly speaking, "Hittite culture" is the term for the mix of the indigenous Hatti - culture and the Semitic culture of the Assyrians.

8

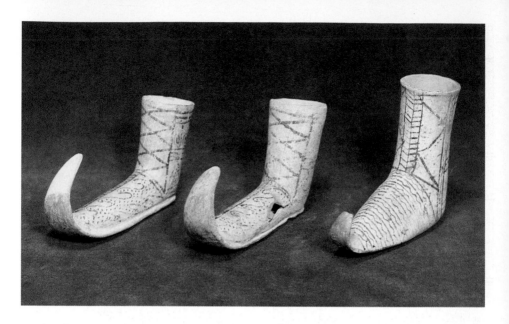

In the second era of that period, (from 1800 BC) a style emerged in Central Anatolia which would later become known as "Hittite style." Its existence and influence lasted for centuries. The principal city during the period of the Assyrian Trading Colonies was the city of Nesa or Kanish, the seat of the ancient Kingdom of Kanish, which is today known as Kültepe and situated 21 kilometres north east of Kayseri.

The city of Kültepe is 500 metres from end to end and rises 20 metres above the level of the surrounding plain. This mound was inhabited by local Anatolians and was surrounded by a trading district measuring 2.5 kilometres across, where Assyrian traders lived. The Karum was established towards the end of the third millennium B.C. and there are four building levels I - IV of which the latest is divided into two sub-levels (Ia and b). Cuneiform tablets inscribed in the Old Assyrian dialect of Akkadian were discovered at levels II and Ib. The dates for level II have been put at 1920-1840 B.C. and level Ib at 1810-1740 BC; both levels were destroyed by fire. The documents found provide detailed information about trade between Assyria and Anatolia; they give vivid accounts of loans, interest rates, agreements, transportation contracts, deposits of goods, memoranda of inventories, deposits, and settlements of accounts. Letters deal with public and private and business matters, marriage and divorce, inheritance and the slave trade and they also record court judgments and correspondence with local lords. Among these written documents there are a small number of literary works and school exercise texts. At level Ib the

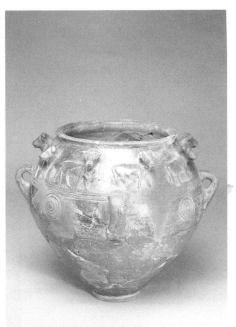

number of tablets found decreases, but despite the decline in trade with Assyria, the city lost none of its wealth and importance. On the city mound, the remains of the monumental palaces of the Kings of Kanish which had been destroyed in a large fire, were discovered.

One of these palaces was situated in the citadel of Kültepe. At ground level, it had 60 rooms, in which clay tablets bearing royal correspondence were discovered. It belonged to Warsama, the son of King Inar of Kanish. A similar palace building was discovered in Acemhöyük near present day Aksaray. In that palace, as well as impression made from the cylinder seals of the famous old Syrian and northern Mesopotamian rulers, there are also exquisitely beautiful art objects made of ivory, rock crystal and gold, which bear clear testimony to the lively trading links between those lands. In this period, stamp seals were used by the indigenous people, which show a particular richness in motifs of a highly developed style.

Another important kingdom of that era was the kingdom of Kussara, whose whereabouts have not been firmly established to date. Two kings of Kussara, Pithana, and his son Anitta, tried very hard to unite the city states and managed to gain control of the most important of them.

Anitta, who captured Hattusa, the capital of the Hatti Kingdom, destroyed and cursed the city with the words, "Whoever becomes king from this time forth, if he settles in the city of Hattusa, he shall be annihilated by the storm god of heaven."

Despite this curse, the city was rebuilt by Labarna, the first king of the Hittite dynasty, and was made the capital of the kingdom. At that time during period of the Assyrian trading colonies, Anatolian art reached a high point. In the palaces of the rulers of Kültepe, Acemhöyük, and in the discovered buildings of Boğazköy and Ališar, hundreds of objects have been found which illustrate the high level attained in all forms of art, architecture and seals, and statuettes made of metal, ivory and ceramics.

At that time, cities emerged in cen-

tral Anatolia that were surrounded by fortified walls. In the most important ones, near official cultic and secular buildings, other structures such as town squares, streets and channels have been unearthed, which allow one to understand the layout and plan of the city. The figurative art and the production of ceramics rose to a new level of creativity. The most important examples of the artwork of this period are the ivory statuettes of a fertility goddess, sphinxes, eagles in flight and animals lying down, and rock crystal statuettes of lions. There are also monochrome and polychrome libation vessels in the forms of people and animals with geometrical patterns, and vases decorated with birds and stylised trees, as well as cosmetics boxes made of ivory and precious stone in the form of pigs, bulls and lions. Along side the Old-Assyrian, Old-Babylonian and Syrian stamp seals are objects fashioned in the indigenous Anatolian style, which are of special significance. On these are processions of gods standing on their animals, religious scenes, scenes of hunting and fighting. They are important because they give prominence to the richness of Anatolian motifs and depictions of religious themes. Libation rhytons in the form of animals and small flat statuettes of gods and goddesses of lead depict the most significant Anatolian goddess with her consort, the chief god, and their children. These were cast in stone moulds.

Pithana, the father of Anitta, and king of Kussara, captured Nesa after a strong attack by night and took its king prisoner, but treated the population as though they were his own flesh and blood; he did them no harm. It is well established that Anitta had temples built in Nesa. This is evident from his text which follows here in a translation by E. Neu:

und in Nesa befestigte ich die Stadt: Nach der Stadt (Befestigung) baute ich einen Temple für den Wettergott des Himmels und einen Tempel für unseren Gott Sine.

Einen Temple für Halmasuit, einen Temple für Wettergott, meinen Herrn, und einen Temple für unseren Gott Sine baute ich. Welches Gut ich von den Feldzugen heimbrachte, damit stattete ich sie aus.

(...and in Nesa I fortified the city; after (fortifying) the city I built a temple for the weather god of heaven and a temple for our god Sine.

A temple for Halmasuit, a temple for the weather god my Lord and a temple for our god Sine were what I built.

Whatever goods I brought home from the battle, I used that to furnish them).

The building level represented by the Nesa Temples (Karum Ib) is contemporary with Anitta, The temples discovered in Nesa are the strongest candidates for identification with the temples which Anitta states he had built in Nesa. Moreover, on a bronze spearhead carv-

ing bearing the cuneiform inscription of Anitta (E - Gal A - ni - ta ru - ba - im = palace of Anitta, the King) was found in situ on the floor of a large room used as a storage unit for unworked obsidien in a rectangular building with which it is contemporary. This building was damaged in a fire, in which the spearhead of Anitta was also burnt.

The burning and ruin of the temples and palaces on the city mound, and of the towns of the Karum and of Kanish, especially of levels II and Ib were caused by the prolonged conflicts and wars that took place between Anatolian rulers themselves. They were not caused by Assyrian traders, who must have stayed out of these conflicts.

As I have pointed out before, with the help of the Kültepe discoveries, it

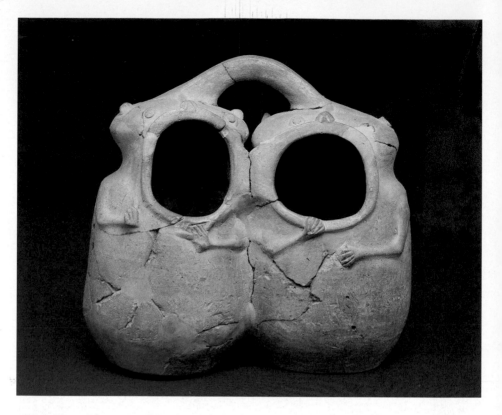

will be possible to explain the meeting of these different influences, the interchange of foreign elements and the distinctive qualities of early Anatolian Hittite art. The relation between the two different peoples living in Kanish was one of harmonious friendship in which their cultures found the chance to develop in peaceful understanding for more than two centuries. The native ethnic group was the Hatti, who created the central Anatolian art of the Assyrian colony period, and the somewhat earlier art of the last quarter of the third millennium B.C. The second group consisted of the Assyrian traders. The cross fertilisation resulting from the contact between the Hatti people, who were the representatives of the native Anatolian civilisation, and the Assyrians, who worked in the ancient Babylonian style of art gave birth to a new mode of expression. It was the origin of what we call Hittite art, that is, the art of the alien Indo-European ethnic group, which was already present in the country during the flourishing period of the Assyrian colonies. Kültepe represents the beginnings of Hittite art, which flourished in the latter half of the second millennium BC, that is, in the period of Great Hittite Empire. The charac-

teristic art of the Hittite Empire, the monumental art of Boğazköy-Hattusa, and Alacahöyük, developed gradually from the representations of the minor art of the Assyrian Trading Colony period. But the Hittites, with their dynamic ability, assimilated the art they found in Anatolia and transformed it into their own individual form of expression. The unique creations bore the imprints of their own identity and are known as Hittite art.

Following his successes, Anitta transferred the centre of his administration from Kussara to Nesa, which he extended. It is of great historical significance that all the greatest Hittite kings of the following era were proud of having descended from "the man from Kussara." Kussara and Nesa were the two greatest capitals and the first to be settled by the Hittites, who had not originally been native to Anatolia, and who had probably immigrated there from the East via the Caucasus. The Hittites called their own language "Nasili," after the name of the city, "Nesa."

This first period of Anatolian history was followed by those of the old and middle Anatolian kingdoms (1600 - 1430 BC). The first great king of that time was Labarna I (of the first half of the 16th century BC). He extended the boundaries of the kingdom,

organised the state and founded a political union in Central Anatolia. Both the kings of that time and those of the following period of the Hittite kingdoms used the name Labarna as a title. Labarna's son Hattusilis (towards the middle of the 16th century BC) also proved with his victory over the kingdom of Aleppo the might of the Hittite state vis-a-vis what was then the most powerful state in the Near East. A surviving testament by this king, which was drawn up in two languages, sheds light on the history of that time. Hattushilis's son Mursilis (of the second half of the 16th century BC), the greatest king of that era, conquered first Aleppo and then Babylon, thereby ending the might of the great Hammurabi dynasty. This important event in history is also reflected in the development of Hittite culture. Following on from this glorious

time was a period of palace intrigues, crime and unrest within the administration. Their dominance over Northern Syria could not be sustained. Telipinus, who was king under these conditions, (1525 - 1500) succeeded in restoring calm and protecting his kingdom from external attack. His greatest achievement was the law of succession by inheritance, which he bequeathed to the Hittite dynasty. The time of Telepinus reign is followed by a "dark age" in Hittite history which lasts for about a hundred years.

The Hittite art of the old and middle kingdoms continued the style of indigenous art from the time of the Assyrian trading colonies. In this period, the Hittites used not only the cuneiform script brought over from Old Babylonia, but also a picture script (hieroglyphics) of their own. A great advance is notice-

able in the typical Hittite seals with their pictures and inscriptions, the drink containers in the forms of bodies of animals, and especially in the occurrences of religious themes, with successive movement, of reliefs of gods, people and animals, as well as on the vases in the forms of animals and the statuettes in metal and ivory and in the ceramics. The indigenous style reveals its Anatolian character in every form of artwork. The large vases of this era decorated with reliefs are some of the most expressive objects surviving from that time.

A relief vase, which came from came from one of the storerooms of the Inandıktepe temple (109 kilometres north of Ankara) is one of the finest examples of Old Hittite pottery. (Fragments of similar relief vases have been unearthed at Bitik, Boğazköy, Eskiyapar and Alişar). It has an oval shaped body with 4 handles, a high neck and a flaring rim; the rim was hollow and libation, passed in though a special opening, flowed into the body of the vase through the mouths of four bulls' heads. The neck and the body are decorated with figured reliefs in four registers separated from one another by hands of geometric motifs. The faces, hands and legs of the figures are painted red, their long hair is black and they are dressed in creamy

yellow or black garments. Most of the figures are shown in profile, but a few have their torsos shown frontally with their hands and legs in profile. The figures have large pointed noses, almond-shaped eyes, small mouths, thick lips and well defined, beardless chins. Though small, the figures are vivid and well - proportioned so that they give a surprising impression of monumentality.

In the first and lowest frieze several scenes are shown: the manufacture of vessels for use in a ceremony, gods seat-

ed on either side of an altar, musicians playing large and small lyres, cymbals and a lute, and people preparing food for a ceremony. In the second frieze a bull is sacrificed before a statue of a bull (the sacred animal of the storm god), votive offerings are brought, under the guidance of secondary gods accompa-nied by a lyre player, and libations are poured before a god who is seated in front of altar. The third frieze shows

male and female deities seated on a bed in front of altar, and processions of men and women moving towards a temple in the company of cymbal players. In the fourth and topmost frieze there are an erotic scene, and a scene of musicians with cymbals, lyres and lutes and acrobats; here the common people are celebrating the sacred marriage depicted in the third frieze.

There is no written document for a Hittite sacred marriage ceremony and the Inandıktepe vase is the first evidence of its existence. The temple of Inandıktepe suffered conflagration in which the vase was also burnt. This is the oldest of the Hittite temples. The weather god on the vase shows his importance of the in the ritual of the sacred marriage, and tells us that Inandıktepe was a city of his cult. This temple is also dedicated to the weather god, who has a multitude of different personalities.

The tablet with the land grant was discovered in one of the storage jars. Its text is written in Akkadian and, Hittite cuneiform script. It had been deposited in the temple by the recipient to be kept in a sacred place.

33

From the Akkadian-Hittite text of Hattushili I we know that the king brought booty from the Euphrates region and Northern Syria and dedicated it in three temples in Hattusa-Boğazköy, the temple of the sun goddess of Arinna, Mezulla and the weather god. This text proves that Hattusa had temples as old as the temple of Inandıktepe.

According to the cuneiform tablet the temple dates back to the time of Hattushili I. The small objects (pottery, terracotta bull statues, stamp seals and a terracotta model of a shrine containing a seated naked figure of a deity) support this idea.

These finds are some of the most outstanding art objects from the period between the old - Assyrian trading colonies and Hittite Empire: their depictions provide us with detailed information about the forms that worship of the gods took and about cult ceremonies. Some of most splendid examples of this style are the small bronze statuettes of the gods, stamp seals and in particular the fragment of an orthostat, which portrays a battle of the gods, statuettes of bulls, and the sacred animals of the weather god.

The vessels are divided into strips and are adorned with painted reliefs. The reliefs on one vase depict a sacred wedding and related scenes. The bottom strip portrays the wedding preparations. Above that, in one strip, a proces-

sion of men and women approach a bull and in another, a bull is sacrificed. In two other strips, two phases of the sacred wedding itself are depicted. A procession of priests and priestesses leading to a temple is also shown. Taking part in the sacred wedding are musicians, dancers and acrobats. The vase dates back to the reign of Labarna Hattushili I. These finds are some of the most outstanding art objects from the period between the old Assyrian trading colonies and the Hittite Empire. Their depictions provide us with detailed information about the forms that worship of the gods took and about cult ceremonies. Some of the most splendid examples of the Hittite style are some small bronze statuettes of the gods, stamp seals and in particular the fragment of an orthostat, which portays a battle of the gods and statuettes of bulls, and the sacred animals of the weather god.

This art is homogeneous and common to the whole of central Anatolia. One can see the style of this period in all its details in the works in the great Hittite centre of Boğazköy, in nearby Alacahöyük, and in Eskiyapar and Inandık (between Kalecik and Çankırı).

Following this period is the time of the Hittite Empire (1430 - 1200). The thousands of cuneiform tablets found in the archives of Boğazköy and the archives of Tel-el-Amarna in Egypt

cast light on the history of that time. Along with these two, a great palace and an archive have in recent years been discovered at Masat Höyük, (in ancient times called Tapigga) which is located 20 kilometres south of Zile (the ancient Zela - Anziliya) and 312 kilometres to the north of Ankara. The archive, the first Hittite one outside Boğazköy, contains tablets of cuneiform inscriptions. The palace too is, after Boğazköy, the first monumental Hittite palace building whose the foundations have been fully excavated.

Then the diplomatic language was Akkadian. At that time, the Hittite kingdom was one of the three great powers of the ancient world. The other two were Egypt and Babylon. Throughout their history the Hittites had consistently shown great interest in Northern Syria. Both Tuthalya, who ascended to the throne in the year 1400 BC, and those who succeeded him until the year 1380 BC, constantly tried to maintain this tradition. However, those who were then ruling Northern Syria, the Mitanni Kings, did not allow them to succeed. At the time of Tuthalya II (1400 - 1380), Boğazköy fell into enemy hands. It was overrun and burnt down by the Gasga, who came from the coast of the Black Sea. The palace of Masat Höyük was built by King Tuthalya II. The city was also built up into a bastion on the frontier against the Gasga. In spite of that, this large city and its palace were captured and destroyed by this merciless enemy from the north. The ascent to the throne of Suppiluliuma I (1380 - 1346) altered the course of Hittite history. Suppiluliuma, who was not only a formidable commander in the field, but also a great statesman, became singlehandedly the founder of the Hittite Empire. After he had restored peace in Anatolia and united the Gasga and other Anatolian peoples under his dominion, and with his back now secured, he began his march on Syria. The Mitanni state disappeared from sight, Aleppo was now conquered and the Hittites were approaching Damascus. Up to that point, the Hittite kings had enjoyed friendly relations with Egypt. That friendship was now about to be shattered. The childless, widowed queen of Egypt wrote a letter to Suppiluliuma asking him to send her one of his sons to be her consort. The murder of the prince before his arrival in Egypt, who had set off only after much debate and doubt, provoked Suppiluliuma into mounting a military campaign against Egypt.

Suppiluliuma's son Mursilis II (1345 - 1315) is also considered one of the great kings of the Hittite Empire. The young king succeeded in suppressing the unrest which broke out upon the death of his father and in restoring security and unity in Anatolia. He conquered the kingdoms to the west of his country and quelled the uprisings in Syria. During the reign of Muwattali, who succeeded his father to the throne (1315 - 1282), the greatest battle in the history of the Egyptians and Hittites took place. This was the battle of Kadesh

(1296). The cause of this conflict was the rivalry over Syria which existed between the two great states. We have no knowledge of the fate of King Muwattali; it is possible that he met his death in the battle of Kadesh. The son who took his place, Mursilis III (1282 - 1275) was deposed by his uncle, Hattushilis III (1275 - 1250). Hattushilis III was a statesman, who achieved great success in politics and administration. The empire reached its full bloom. Every part of the land was built upon and adorned with monuments. Great value was placed on friendly relations between the great states, and with the completion of a peace treaty, an end to the 17-year-long war with Egypt was prepared. The text of this treaty, which has survived down to us, is the oldest example of a defence and mutual aid pact between two states. Also and for this reason, a copy of it has been placed in the United Nations building. The pact is drawn up upon the basis of the full equality of rights of both partners.

Hattushili III's son Tuthalya IV (1250 - 1220) also ranks as one of the powerful kings of the empire, and his mother Pudu-Hepa is one of the most significant figures in Hittite history. During the reign of this king and queen, the Hittite cult was reorganised, and sculpture and the interpretative arts reached their highest point. Yet, at the same time, the great king was forced to come to terms with the Assyrian king to the east and the small western Anatolian kingdoms in the west. After the death of Tuthalya IV, his son Arnuwanda III (1220 - 1190) became king. Now saw

45

the rise of movements and revolutions against the Hittite realm in Western Anatolia. We have no records of the activities of this king, whose reign was beset by the menacing signs of dangers. However, through newly discovered documents, it has been established that the last of the Hittite kings was not Arnuwanda but Suppiluliuma II (around 1190). During the period of his reign, the empire collapsed under the onslaught of the sea peoples, who flooded in from the west across the sea in giant waves -- the so-called Aegean migration. The capital at Boğazköy with its city walls and castles, which had been considered impregnable, was overrun and burnt down; Hittite cuneiform was never used again. About the race which had made its mark on the most significant time span of ancient Anatolia's cultural history, all documents now fall silent.

The art of this period is typical of that of an empire. Hittite art is above all a religious and royal art. All cities, especially the capital Boğazköy, were made secure by fortresses and consolidated at strategic points, which were at that time unassailable. The Hittites succeeded in constructing the most powerful military architecture in the Near East. The gates of the fortresses were embellished with reliefs of lions, sphinxes and gods and the inner fortresses and citadels were particularly reinforced.

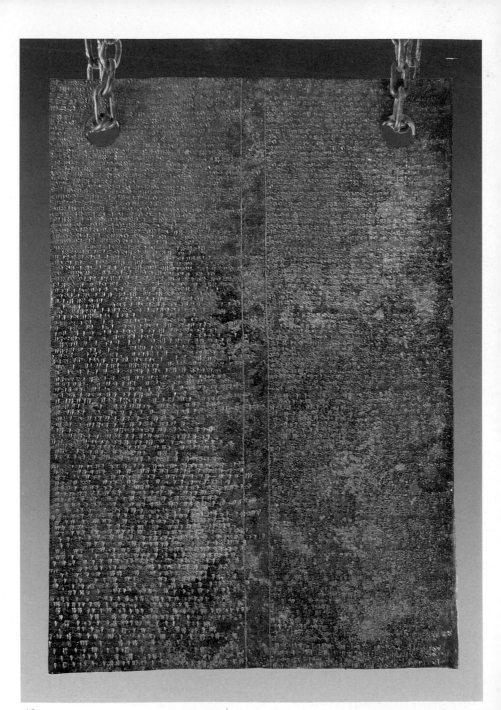

48

The subterranean passage ways, which were built with the false-arch technique, and the poterns and great stairways survive to this day in Boğazköy, Alacahöyük, Gavurkale (between Ankara and Haymana) as memorials to Hittite military architecture.

The city gates and shrines were adorned with orthostats and upright monuments embellished with reliefs; in the cities, large state shrines were built.

The temples in Boğazköy have the character of great complexes; the the shrine to the weather god is typical with its length of 160 metres and its breadth of 135 metres, its spacious layout, its wide courtyards, its large windows and abundant store rooms.

The Hittite cult buildings, whose plans are basically symmetrical, are one type of buildings particular to the Hittites. In contrast to the customs of other ancient peoples, the cult practices of the Hittite sanctuaries took place in the daylight, in the open air.

The Hittite temples with their depots, archives living quarters and holi-

form of a procession. Through these cult pictures, our knowledge of the polytheistic beliefs of the Hittites and the Hittite forms have been extraordinarily enriched. Among the figures a group, in which the king is embraced by the god Sarruma, is a masterpiece of this style. The Hittite great kings used to have figures of the gods and kings carved with hieroglyphic inscriptions in reliefs on rock slabs on the places they conquered and along the strategic roads along which they marched. They also had hieroglyphic inscriptions carved at the water reservoirs and fountains they built or the surroundings of the springs that they had made accessible. Furthermore, the metal and ivory statuettes, which have been found in different centres of Anatolia, the seals of kings and other people, and the cuneiform documents give us abundant information about the art, history, religion, administration and all forms of the daily life of the Hittites. The statuettes of the gods and goddesses have the same characteristics of style as those of the rock reliefs. On the stamp imprints of the Hittite great kings the name of the king was given both in hieroglyphic script and in cuneiform. We see in the rock reliefs in Yazılıkaya and elsewhere the depiction of the king and queen, with their cartridges found nearby. There are also depictions of gods and goddesses receiving offerings. Not far away, depictions of gods also appear without inscriptions. One such depiction shows the scene of an introduction of a prince with mountain gods standing on bulls, and another shows a weather god in his chariot on three mountain gods, which is being pulled by genies. These

est parts furnished with statues of the gods give a vivid picture of the concept of architecture at that time. In the citadel of Boğazköy, which is called "Büyükkale" - Great Fortress - in which the kings had their place of residence, the finest examples of the official Hittite architecture the state archives and the reception halls have been uncovered. "Yazılıkaya," which lies 2 kilometres northeast of Boğazköy, is a Hittite open air sanctuary, a Hittite pantheon. Here, 83 figures have been carved out of the rock face. All male and female deities of the Hittite empire are depicted in the

rank among the most vivid of the mythological depictions.

In the town of Alacahöyük, there is the Sphinx gate, which at that time served as a city gate. It is adorned to the left and right with orthostats from the 14th century, which depict the following: a king and queen praying, a man bringing four goats, a person approaching a seated god, two people climbing on ladders, and near to that a sword swallower, musicians, the worship of a god seated on a throne, and deer and boar hunting. A bull relief, which originates from Alacahöyük, and which very graphically and vigorously depicts a bull in the moment of its charge, and the masterful high relief of a god which earlier adorned a city gate in Boğazköy, are some of the most beautiful Hittite works of art. The Hittites are the people who founded the first large city in Central Anatolia and left their monumental art work, which has survived to our own day. When as a result of a huge onslaught the Hittite state suddenly ceased to exist, the Hittites who emigrated to the regions of the East Taurus and Southeast Anatolia reestablished small kingdoms in the region from which they had first originated, nearly in the region of Malatya near to Karkamish, which was at its time a large Hittite centre, as well as in Maraş (Gurgum) and Zincirli (Sam'al). These kingdoms used the Hieroglyphic script and continued the Hittite style in that region. Nevertheless, they never united to form one state.

The region which extended from the

Karkamish, Maraş (Gurgum) and Zincirli, which had already for some time been ruled by an Aramaean dynasty. The art of that time can be divided by style and form into three periods: the first of these encompasses the time before 950, the second period between 950 and 850, and the third the eighth century BC. The orthostats which adorned the gate of Malatya come closest in context, style and motifs to the Hittite art of the empire. In the eighth century BC, the influence of Assyrian art made itself very strongly felt. The best representative of this is the 3.18 metre - high statue of the king of Milid (Malatya), which is found in the Museum of Anatolian Civilisations.

In the second period of late-Hittite art, one finds substantially more orthostats, which are on a larger scale than previously. They portray the following motifs: animals, demons, lords of the animals, gods standing on lions, hybrid creatures (half man, half lion) gryphons, beings with the heads of birds, mythical scenes, sphinxes, a procession of men and women and those of the goddess Kubaba seated on a throne, the goddess who is already known to us from Kültepe. In all these scenes, one finds the style of the art work of the Hittite empire one finds on a large scale. In this period, pictures and scripts are employed next to each other and form a composite whole. In the last period, one sees the Assyrian influence starting to predominate, and the traces of the old style becoming so weak as to be almost indiscernible. The orthostats dating from 760, which depict Kamanas, the son of King Araras of Karkemis, are considered the most interesting exam-

mid Kızılırmak (Halys) area to Mid-Syria and Konya and had formed the southern and southeastern part of the Hittite empire, was later ruled over by the new or late Hittite city states. In this region, there are examples of late Hittite figurative art of between the tenth and eighth centuries in many places, but there are four centres of particular importance. These are Malatya,

ples of this period. These orthostats also exhibit very beautiful non-religious motifs. The orthostats of Karkemis form the richest collection in the Museum of Anatolian Civilisations in Ankara.

In Cylicia there are very provincial orthostats, which embellished the gates of Karatepe near Kadirli. They date from the end of the eighth century BC. The motifs here are mostly Aramaic and Phoenician, and are outside the Anatolian tradition. The orthostats, which adorned the late-Hittite palace in Sakçagözü, belong to the end of the eighth century as well. Most of these are also on display in the Museum of Anatolian Civilisations.

Exposed to the attacks and raids of the Assyrians, who by that time had become much - stronger, these kingdoms, which were also coming under Assyrian influence in their art, began one after another, to disappear from sight, and by around the year 700 BC the Hittites were fully under the overlordship of the Assyrians. Nevertheless, these kingdoms had succeeded in preserving the Hittite style and hieroglyphic script up until that time, in spite of all outside influences.

The works of art of those cultural times and periods, which we have endeavoured to describe, are for the most part on display in the Museum of Anatolian Civilisations in Ankara and the Archaeology Museum in Istanbul; and some are also in the local museums of Boğazköy, Alacahöyük, Kayseri, Adana, Maraş, Karatepe and Gaziantep.